Robert Conway is a career trial attorney and litigator. He makes his living by oratory expostulation, exhortation, emphasis, alliteration, repetition, metaphor, and crescendo.

He composes, his written word in this rhythm, in this rhyme and in this phrasing, with this pulse and grandeur of the well-turned phrase.

He is a successful lawyer, happily married to his first and only wife, Katherine. He dedicates his writing to his wife, to his three daughters and grandchildren.

I dedicate this writing to Katherine Conway, the great love of my life, and to our three daughters, the flowers of our love.

Robert Conway

THE DEMONIC

AUSTIN MACAULEY PUBLISHERS
LONDON • CAMBRIDGE • NEW YORK • SHARJAH

Copyright © Robert Conway 2024

All rights reserved. No part of this publication may be reproduced, distributed, or transmitted in any form or by any means, including photocopying, recording, or other electronic or mechanical methods, without the prior written permission of the publisher, except in the case of brief quotations embodied in critical reviews and certain other non-commercial uses permitted by copyright law. For permission requests, write to the publisher.

Any person who commits any unauthorized act in relation to this publication may be liable to criminal prosecution and civil claims for damages.

Ordering Information
Quantity sales: Special discounts are available on quantity purchases by corporations, associations, and others. For details, contact the publisher at the address below.

Publisher's Cataloging-in-Publication data
Conway, Robert
The Demonic

ISBN 9798889102021 (Paperback)
ISBN 9798889102038 (Hardback)
ISBN 9798889102045 (ePub e-book)

Library of Congress Control Number: 2024901498

www.austinmacauley.com/us

First Published 2024
Austin Macauley Publishers LLC
40 Wall Street, 33rd Floor, Suite 3302
New York, NY 10005
USA

mail-usa@austinmacauley.com
+1 (646) 5125767

So grand the dream that tempests in the mind,
That cries its theater in one's sleep confined.

A truth strains to announce its essence here,
That from its tethered realm subsistence flow.

So swells the thought,
The all-triumphant thought,
That in mind's visions clarions out its truth.
Hie to me this self-most thought,
This winnowed, frail, and near-still stilling thought.

In storied fashion told the truth its tale
Within the darkling drama of this dream,
Where none the logic, nor the rule prevail;
So banished law and all the order seem.
This parable was ushered to the fore
And strung its storied steps across night's stage.
The host it prisoned and his person kept,
Churning his upheaval while he slept.

This night was shadowed as I walked alone.
Down somber paths which clouds so grim beset.
A chill was shivered through one's breast and bone;
The cobbles dripped with rain and frigid sweat.
Lurid darkness paced with me my path,
And swarthy leaden stillness dragged its cloak.
The night was laden heavy in its air;
Misty dullness swelled and leaped its lair.

The shadow fall was soundless as I walk,
Stifling every breath I stuttered out.
Blackness on my hind-step came to stalk,
And silence overwhelm me with its shout.
The air unmoved, hung sullen, curtain-like,
Resisting every tremor in its breast.
Thickly was the night suffused and swollen,
As if life with the passing day was stolen.

The sound was strangled, choking as it move,
Dying when its vibrance night remove.

The silence surged and wrapped me in its arms.

Cradling, curdling,
Smothering, girdling,
It drank in every sound.

The draught was downed,
The murmur drowned,
A stillness trumpet song.

The voice was mummed.

A pregnant hush was anchored to the ground.

I, beneath stillness breast.
        Leapt in the womb.

Within the templed night I set my pace.
I chanced to be about on business way.
Willingly I welcomed dark's embrace,
Passed I in the night as if were day.
Pressing 'gainst the turgid wall of night,
I pull my mantle tightly 'round my throat.
Mournful stride I stepped in starless stage;
The night streamed on and flowed in quiet rage.

Water paint the boots upon my feet,
That kicked the flood sheets lying on the street.

My hand was pulled across my faceless face,
Holding out the cold with but my shirt.
The tunic to my cloak I tightly lace;
A cord around my waist was fastly girt.
Night's chilled fingers ran upon my back,
And pricked the skin it kissed upon my chest.
Around my head was pulled and drawn my hood,
Clinging to my cheeks as cold withstood.

Weaponless I course my path this night,
Armed with but a purse and bits of gold.
Unarmored did I pass, so little fright,
But night brought quaking with its numbing cold.
Quicken did my stammered pulse and heart.
Quickly did the ground pass 'neath my feet.
The dungeon night encaged me in its dark,
Crawling on my flesh as bare and stark.

The night ran fast as I,
And still more so.
I couldn't pace,
Or near outrace its realm.

It fingered me
And pressed its palm across my eyes.

Everything was sightless,
Without a glow
Everything was brightless.
I tumbled on and stumbled on.

Everywhere the same.
I have passed a mile,
And passed a mile then twice.
Passed another.
Passing then for thrice.

Still away, so away,
From where one wished to be.

This night and I were not so much alone.
A man's foot set his heel upon the ground.
Tossing stillness from its somber throne,
It cry intents and chased me as a hound,
One pursuer summoned him another,
Calling still a third to join the hunt.
The mongrel-hearted pack with cursing came,
Crying depredations, wants and shame.

Fled I through the sable-coated tunnel.
Fled I past and down the pitchy walls.
I hurl myself into the blackened funnel,
Through the inky, unflecked, sunless halls.
They cried and told me just to drop my purse,
And if it fell no need had I to fear.
Upon my coinage pouch I placed my hand,
Swearing at the still-pursuing band.

The money was for purchase in the mart,
Wherein was I in high regard and proud,
Where contracts made and I was to be part.
I bargains made, agreed, partook, allowed.
Here there was no marketplace to mingle.
The thieves sought for my gold but not for me.
Across the fallen timbers tracks elude,
But yet the hare was still hard-pressed, pursued.

I shifted, shunted, sheered within the wood.
Every twist and swerve the pack withstood.

The gnarling-fingered trees ripped at my face;
Reeds and roots ensnared my passing foot.
The webbing cords of night enwrapped their lace,
Beneath my stride the stumble-block it put.
A thousand thicket hands grabbed at my cloak,
The columned trees pressed in to wall my path
Night was seething, clutching at me here,
Unmoving while the highwaymen drew near.

Sedge and bullrush cordoned as I passed,
Relentless in the clutch it set about.
The shrub and brake entwine the fleer fast.
Brassy-voiced this hare let wretched shout.
My eyes were swept away with tearful tide.
I screamed and cried and begged for freedom's field.
These arms were by the rushes side-bound lashed;
I forward pushed and tossed and downward crashed.

Whimpering my all too-quickened breath,
I cursed and wept at my entombing death.

Feverish trembling closed my paining eyes;
Shivering hands scratched out to maim the skies.

With sticks and rods they beat me to my feet.
My face was slashed, and spat upon and whipped.
They damned and oathed and damns again repeat;
Their hands around my whining throat were gripped.
My back was struck and struck and struck again.
The cloak was ribboned by the switches cut.
From one the other boastingly I fell,
Legless, handless, prisoned in this spell.

A scourge was twist from brambles and the thorns,
Spine and needle bristling from the branch.
By hand this prick and briared barb was borne,
Splaying out the blood I tried to stanch.
The spurred and thistly whip ripped at my flesh,
Painting me with welts and trails of blood.
They dragged its tail across my legs and chest,
Sewing rows of bloodlines on my breast.

I begged for cease.
They laughed for more.
I cried for peace.
They beat the more.

Clinging to the ground I cried for death.
I crawled upon the earth.
I mourned my very birth.

The pain, the swell, the throb, the gnaw;
Their lash, their fists, their wooden claw.

I lie there still
      And feel no more.

My blood was rushing river-full and free
From off my brow, and matted up my hair.
I couldn't move to try to rise to flee.
My breath was heavy, laden, barely there.
They kicked and prodded, searching for response;
No muscle nor a sinew cared to leap.
A breathing death I lay, a throttled hulk,
Lying lifeless, slaughtered, butchered bulk.

No movement for an instant did torment me.
They laugh that by their strength they all but spent me.

A hand reached to my belt and pulled it loose;
My gold fell free and danced upon the ground.
It splayed and rolled and fled its leather noose,
A golden-throated chinking tinkled 'round.
The gilded pieces clinked and jingled down;
Silver sterling also loosed and drop.
Every coin had fallen tumbling free.
Spilled upon the blooded earth it be.

A cry, a ring of satisfaction rose,
Bounding through the nightly-hooded wood.
Through cathedral forest halls it flows,
And echoed in night's chambers where they stood.
Every piece of mint they clutched and held,
Sifting for my coinage in the dirt.
Among themselves they fought to have the most,
And bandied 'bout their claims and stealing's boast.

They took their all unsacred coins and left,
Sated by profane, unhallowed theft.

My mind into a groaning darkness fell;
The brigands from the bramble fled away.
A swirling tempest tossed me in its hell,
And pitched me in its rankish crests and sway.
Caged within my mind, I wished to run,
But nowhere was escape to show its door.
My soul, now disembodied, slowly drifts,
And sank or rose by paining's waves or lifts.

A throbbing ache upon my eyes was set,
Burning at the vaguest hint of light.
It scolded every movement with regret,
And tar-smeared every flickering of light.
Indicting every sense as being crazed,
It hurled the quilted conscious to convulse.
A pounding beat within my paining skull
That only thoughtless death or sleep could dull.

The demons came and danced within my brain,
Torching and en-firing what remain.

A blazing, bristling pyre all consumed.
Every thought and sense to ashes fell.
The fires leaped and burnished columns flumed,
A bounteous mind collapsed within its shell.
A frenzied immolation burned my strength;
Memory was charred to no recall.
Gentleness was victim to the flame.
My courage, worth and kindness died the same.

Virtue lingered, succumbing last of all,
Crying out its name through ruined halls.

Malignance set its banner on the heap
That by the doleful furies was enwrapped.
Triumphantly it pranced it ramping leap,
As all the dire spirits raged and flapped.
The wraith, it cackled on the pile of dead,
The simple goodness lying at his feet.
He perched upon my sunken, lifeless chest,
And sank its claws into the fallen breast.

This legion in my mind I sought to rise,
Climbing to my knee with tumored pain.
The vision flared and blinded in my eyes;
Every muscle screamed to end its strain.
My trumpet gave this anarchy reprise,
Shaking at the pillars of my mind.
Riot in my soul had sought its run;
Chaotic ferment webbed, and wrapped, and spun.

My hands upon my face reached for the pain,
Trying to excise it from my mind.
Still ten thousand fires brand my brain,
Scorching every tranquil thing it find.
I stand upon my feet and stumble 'round,
Arm outstretched and pleading not to fall.
Vision blackened, thought a putrid mire,
I stood consumed within this parching fire.

Still unseeing, blank-eyed did I sprawl,
Lurching, pitching, always near the fall.

Down the tree-lined cavern did I run,
As far as might from where the deed was done.

A hatred, breathless hatred, welled within,
Spitting curse and outrage at the thieves,
Who did commit this savage violent sin,
Under night-swells heavy blackened eaves.
Tormenting death I cried for such as these,
A death as such not known to men before.
I yearn to see them cry that death be theirs,
But death avoiding, lingers unawares.

I screamed for vengeance,
Dame, bride-like vengeance,
Vengeance to make me whole.

I prayed it,
Upbraid it,
Begged the gods who made it.

Might I have it now.
Might I see them suffer.
May the gold turn molten in their hands.
May it scald their flesh and weld their fingers to a ruck.
May they pain so remorselessly that
Pain have no vent but death.

Let them weep 'til tears will come no more.
Let them scream 'til their voices have no depth.
Let them pain 'til their tortured senses die.

Let them die by my hand.

My eyes are wide but passion strikes them blind,
Consumed in loathing fires burning wild.
Their lives to broken fragments I would grind.
My self-respect by violence they defiled.
A club I lift from near my booted foot,
To part their skull in image execution,
I poise with arm up-raised to strike the blow,
And dream that death to them from my hand flow.

Death moves from what my fingers touch.

But they have fled away.
My rage I rage alone.

The club falls on a faceless block of stone,
Shattering in my hand as down it fall.
Ungodly cry from out my throat has flown,
And fled into the rotted wooded hall.
The shards of wood exploded on the rock,
That sternly broke the bludgeon on its back.
Splinters fired in the raging dark,
And flighted like a wounded wing in air.

I had done the deed.
The stone had died beneath the blow.
Tormentors dead;
And I had willed it so.

I laughed and cried that this much I had done.
My wounding wanted killing for its toll.
I had smited out their thieving sun,
And did declare the vengeance of my soul.
A devilish cheer roared deep within my chest.
This image death was mine and mine alone.
I flushed with pregnant, fiendish pride
That death, in dire-face, stood by my side.

But then from out the rushes pushed a face,
To watch me for this moment of my rage.
It saw of me this moment of disgrace,
Cavorting so ungodly on this stage.
It smiled at me an unforgiving smile;
A fiendish glee was writ upon its cheek.
Its eyes were fired with a demon glow;
It glowered out and all its evil show.

It stared at me from there between the reeds,
Smiling at the fool I seemed to be.
He eyed me scarcely hidden in the weeds.
His face and but his face alone I see.
Our eyes had locked in stupefying gaze,
Bewildered, awed, and breathlessly aghast.
The smile was haunting in its too-pleased joy,
That reveled in my wanting to destroy.

The face was fleshless, pale, and honey-bare,
Blanched and white, of ghostly snowy tint.
Matted and disheveled was the hair
That framed the smile that shined like silvered flint.
His eyes were empty, deeper than his skull,
Seizing at my gaze which passed too near.
Gray eyes sat within a face of steel,
Triumphant as the rancored smile reveal.

He glared and hissed to see my frigid spell,
Too harrowed in this place where evil dwell.

The smile,
The all-possessing smile
That snared me,
Shared me,
Near to death it scared me.
It held me,
Wouldn't let me move.

I couldn't look,
And couldn't look away.

It smiled and wanted,
Smiled and had,
Smiled and haunted,
       Deathly-clad.

It courted wildness, frenzy, and decay,
Death and dying, ruin, disarray.

Deranged, distraught, I read within its eyes
Seer, demon, cloaked in mortal lies.

This face I knew. Had often seen before,
The face of madness, terror, and the whore.

So swiftly did it come.
So swiftly did it flee.
One moment was.
One moment gone.
And there it ceased to be.

In fear I stood, still shackled to the ground,
Staring at the place where he had been.
No movement rustled or the slightest sound,
In this unholy, sacrilegious den.
The blackened palace walls pressed tighter in;
More silent grew the darkly cloistered wood.
The reeds were still where recently he hid;
Stealthily, he through the canebrake slid.

With terror wrapped like chain about my heart,
I whirled and sought the face to show again.
I steeled myself lest once again he dart
And race from out the shadows in the glen.
A moan and terrifying plaint I breath,
Searching for the visage in the brush.
The midnight veil had all the forest cloaked.
Every splintered light the darkness choked.

I wheeled and scanned and strained to see the face,
That for that moment lingered in this place.

A horror crept within my heaving breast,
As wondered I, had I, a Satan seen.
The face I knew and, shamedly, knew best,
That portrait, sickened features, low demesne.
I all too simply recognized the beast,
Those harshly leering, glaring, prying eyes.
A demon smile was written on its face,
That to a devil's foundry might I trace.

I knew, I knew. I dare to know that eye.
I knew the smile, the grimace, and the twist,
The knotted lip, the all too limpid wry,
Contorted like a bloodied, swollen fist,
The rough-hewn cheeks, the broken-chisel chin,
A kneaded brow, the slice of uncast nose,
An unmold shapeless mass of facial form,
Malignant as the thunder-wracking storm.

But still the face I knew, the sculpted stamp,
That smiled from out the horrid evening's damp.

The face was MINE.

My every-mirrored face.

I had wrought the demon-ghost I saw.
I bore it, borne it;
My face did there adorn it.
My face appalled me.
Looking at it galled me.
But damnably it thralled me
        When I saw it there.

I sickened with emotion
At the too repulsive notion
        That the face was mine.

More dense then grew the loathsome tragic night,
Baying for a moon or shaft of light,
But begged I for another moment's sight
Of ever-chafing captivating fright.

The wretched thing was me,
The stricken, plaguing, woeful thing was me.

Where was the witching, guiling demon now,
That might my madness to him disavow.

My rampage for the thieves gave him his beckon,
This devil from my unforgiving Self.
He came to set my madness by his reckon,
And set me, ruined treasure, on his shelf.
The burning want to kill had been his summons,
Burgeoned from my soul where it had hid.
He crept as close as frenzy let him come,
Closer yet than ever had he plumb.

In that manic moment we were near,
As close as but an eye-shot glance and peer.

I'd given strength to dare he move to show
My heart distorted in my raging's throe.

If he was a shadow in my soul,
A tumor in the spirit of my life,
I would forsake the evil it extol,
And banish every hatred, lust, and strife.
I'd lay a knife on every limb he claim;
Blank an eye if but he call it his.
The vengeance I exalted was his child;
Revenge and malice call him in its wild

I stroked my face and tossed aside the sweat.
The blood had mixed with dirt to smear it dry.
I pulled at where my tunic was upset,
And draped it 'cross my shoulders hitching high.
My boots and breeches still clung to my leg,
Ripped and torn they covered yet my sores.
My cloak hung down in tatters to the ground;
About my quivering body it was wound.

I gazed into the blackness searching hard
To once again recall my demon seed.
My arms outstretch his near approach to guard,
Lest he should come far closer than was need.
My eye around me surveyed every course,
Each avenue as far as sight would take.
The rustle in the reeds announced him near,
But never did his face break from the drear.

I mumbled out a summons of my name,
Calling out the Self I knew in shame.

A muted fascination took the stead
Of horror but a moment now displaced.
Unknowing shied the paralyzing dread.
The search had numbing terror soon outpaced.
Alert at every muscle, nerve, and sense,
A pitching blade of grass drew careful heed.
I waited for a muffled scrape or slide,
A crack, a rustle, tinkle, hush, or stride.

The stillness swelled.
It boomed, it paled.
Its sharpness cut the dark.

Too thick to let a murmur crease the air,
The prey and preyor parried in night's lair.

I stopped my breath.
No gust or breeze took flight.
No draft or current tossed the turgid night.

The wind was wounded, stilled, near dead.
The silence fill my paining head.
Every Nature's sign I read.

But he was not.
My Self had fled away.

A brittle, grainy, burned-throat laugh I heard,
Far from where I thought the demon be,
A cackle like the strangling of a bird,
Rose from where my wide eye couldn't see.
The laugh was smothered in the laugher's throat,
Choked away, lest someone know his place.
I, for a moment, thought I didn't hear,
The muted hissing hidden in the drear.

But then a simper broke from out its chest,
Spiraling up, a beacon in the shade.
The laughter burst in merriment and zest,
Cutting through the umber in the glade.
I cried my find in cresting exultation,
Screaming at my other horrored Self.
My voice in shapeless tone cry out my place,
And set out in the darkest, dimmest chase.

"I'll find you," did I cheer within the wood,
Racing through the thickets a I could.

With fleeting foot I strided through the dark,
Pursuing but the sound he leave me there.
I coursed my path to where he left a mark,
I, the hound, and he, the fleeting hare,
Bounding through the briar and the brush,
And glancing off the wooded steeple's walls.
I set myself to flight upon the trail,
Pushing through the damask darkened veil.

From where there came the courage was unknown;
But somewhere in my heart was daring sewn.

My own face lured this journeyer to go,
To follow its temptation in the dark,
To know from whence it came and whence it grow,
And why its eye was barren, bare and stark.
Unnatural in attraction was the thing
Spawned of me and nurtured in my breast.
I couldn't let it flee and not be caught,
When every sense and value was distraught.

I must confront the Self I seek again,
Even in his godless, baleful den.

His becking laugh erupted once the more,
Down an eb'ny corridor and hall.
The smutted sky still lapped the starless shore
And hurled its swarthy cloak across the pall.
A lurid, somber heaven watched above
The fast-paced strider and his chase below.
The darkness crowed as if light never be.
A morbid, blackened canvass all we see.

The earth into a soft decline had turned,
Sloping to the downward as I run.
My pace grew faster as I now discerned.
It seemed so far behind I left the sun.
I twist my head to look again aback,
Straining for a bolt of light to see.
But none was there, nor was there none the more.

The dark behind the same as dark before.
The lightlessness cascaded down the path,
Barking at my heels its murky wrath.

I downward chased the lewdly laughing demon.

The steadier foot was ever here the lower.

I heard him still
A space away.
I heard again.
His laugh betray.

I chased him.
Traced him.
Set my tramping, stamping step
        And paced him

But gained I not a step.

Hurly, burly, whirly foot I ran;
Reeling, shallow breath was stealing,
        Ran I on his track.

Pain me.
Strain me.
Every muscle drain me.
But not a step was gained.

My flesh-tied bundled bones with sinew bound
Was not the equal to the leaping hare.

But still I heard
The painful, whining word,
That from his laughing heart was stirred.

I'd heard the laugh before.

In safer sun-kissed times had billowed out
That too pernicious laugh I now pursue.
It robed itself with disbelief and doubt.
Every time I sought the laugh withdrew.
Before I'd seen the tremor in the leaves,
The quiver in the thickets in the vale,
I'd known him there when haunting did he come.
I'd heard his foot and heard his sneering hum.

When selfishness had trumpeted my name,
When lust or passion cried me to their course,
At times when revel took I in my shame,
To scoff at order, gentleness, or laws,
Then would come the titter from the shade,
The throaty gasp that cheered my soul's demise,
Turning would I see the form then swear
That scarce a breath before a man was there.

But never did I once espy the face
That still so far ahead of me I chase.

His foot I'd heard before and laughter. Yes.
But always had he fled to this recess.

A shock of lightning crashed about the sky,
Pointing jagged fingers at the earth.
Its light had tided darkness to deny,
Flinging shaft of brightness all its girth.
Bleaching breakers broke upon the walls
Of rocks and ridges in the sloped defile.
The wood had turned to ashen forest wreck
Of lifeless trees with cracked and slatted neck.

The leaden sky was wracked with warring clouds,
A piled and swollen, wind-drift pallid shroud.

A spine of mountains ridged to left and right.
Granite towers, grim, majestic, rose
To haunch their backs to challenge heavens might.
These unforgiving reefs their shoals expose.
A boney grist was kicking from the summit,
The iron-armored shield that covered earth.
Hoar-frost, ghastly silver painted all,
This pearly, ashy, death-masque smirchen pall.

Tufted, castle-crescent, cliff-lined alleys
Fingered through the toothy headland spur.
The broken forest withered in the valleys
Where nothing lived, or moved, or caused a stir.
The mountains plumed and hurled their ramparts highward
Challenging the tempests in the heavens.
Gnarly, bone-broke notches cut the sky;
Plaited, craggy, ruckered, it defy.

Furrows cut the hillside downs its back;
Ravines and arid bluffs were cut in line,
Guttered where a wat'ry knife had hack,
Rutted, etched, and troughed were down the spine.
Spitted, staved, and pocked by chisel's pick,
The sculptor cut his trenches sorely cruel.
Engraver's hand with ugliness had set
The pitted face he wish the peaks beget.

No waters washed the mountains face or crest.
No leafy life had hillock's bosom blessed.

In but the moment's space when light was rife
Among the dying hills and recess path,
I saw the man-form borne amidst my strife,
Who carried in his breath my primal wrath.
He turned and saw me still a league apart,
Straining with the cane and rubble's wreck.
Again I knew that this his face was mine.
I saw myself in every curve and line.

The laugh was stifled for a moment's term.
The smile, now gone, his face was grimly firm.

His eyes grew wild to see me now so near,
So close to press my hand upon his throat.
A terrored pallor bleached his raging leer.
Anger in his hate had chimed its note.
A gutt'ral baying rumble through his lips,
Crying like the killing of a doe.
In but the lightning's flash our eyes had met,
Chilling like a frosting, frigid sweat.

He turned and ran.
I ran again.
Stumbling, tumbling,
      Falling, ran again.

His cry arose.
His place disclose.
And followed I again.

Burly-breathed he fumed and foamed
That I should so near be.
A roaring shrilling cry he bark.
He knew that I was he.

The footprints here had all been his.
No single man had come.
Unchallenged was he in this world
Which evil he was from.

The laugh was now unpiped.
His yell and clamor sliced the air.
He grunted, moaned,
Shrieked and groaned.

He wailed like a mother whose son's lost life,
Or a man who buries a long-loved wife.
He bleated like a wounded ram,
      Cut with mortal knife.

I dare not for a moment chart my course,
Or ponder what this madding phantom know.
But must I see this presence at its source,
And from what empty hollow it would grow.
My tumor seethed a too malicious life,
Sprouting bile and pregnant with its death.
As manly hearts once wounded pour in flood,
It feasted on the flesh and drank the blood.

Somewhere in my soul I felt his touch.
My own malignance beckoned him arise.
I ushered him to be my demon crutch,
Warring on the good and on the wise.
From where he came so too my heart had come.
The trail down the defile I seemed to know.
The mountains, and the hemorrhaged sky I saw
Was all but too familiar for my awe.

The cliffs encircled every thought I bore,
Bordering mind's valleys and mind's shore.

But that mind was far away
    And scarce remembered here.

Within which trees and blossom sprouted wild,
And gentleness upon that glade was playing,
When the gracious kindness bore its child,
The verdant green was waft in breezes swaying.
In these Elysian fields of human grandeur,
Moved the noblest thoughts a man might bear.
Lofty-hanging mankind brought his peace,
Giving every bounty its increase.

Far away, so very far away.

But here, within abyss's walls, there rose
The spiny, misted, fog-shade sunken lair,
Where kindliness to elements expose,
Withered in the smothered rancid air.
From Paradise of human virtue saw
The backbone of a selfish, rigid lust.
Amidst the deathly wind that press the breeze
Muted storming echoed as it please.

A part of me was minted in that mill,
Forged within this foundry of the will.

The crucible in which my soul was formed,
Had from the molten pitch cast out this man,
In which the Good and Evil authors stormed,
Fashioning their nature as they can.
Each essence grappled with the other there,
Wrestling in unending mortal bout.
One, the garden, one, the desert bare,
One, the hospice, one, the devil's lair.

This other Self I must seek out and find,
If but to know the evil in my mind.

He knew these canyons, chasms, and ravines,
Better than did I who stumbled down.
But still familiar were these ghastly scenes,
That wore the sooty cloak, and sable gown.
In this sepulchral palace hewn of stone,
I was not a stranger but a guest.
He fled me lest I gaze upon my face,
And know too well the plague upon my race.

If this be true than death perhaps I call,
Despairing of the fate that must befall.

From up the cracks and seams
A sulfurous, burning, singeing steam
Cut through the murky dark.
        A dunnish glow had lighted on the stage.

Pallid shadows danced upon the wall.
Flecking, flitting,
Bursting, splitting,
In the death-house halls.

Fires flumed
And pyres spumed,
Burning in the stone.

Lumpish rock cracked in the cruel flame.
Sizzled, hissed,
The blaze was twist,
And never moved the same.

Simmer, smolder, singe, and boil;
Parch, and seethe, and scald, and broil.

The smoke had flood the air,
Stealing breath,
Congealing breath.

Everywhere and everywhere
        And shadows everywhere.

As far as eye could blinking see
His back was turned in flight.

His cloak unfurled and flared upon the wind.
Bare-chested did he down the concourse run.
It seemed a glint about his hip was pinned,
A toneless sparkle winking in the dun.
Swordblade thought I as him I pursue,
A narrow-handled dagger it did seem.
No lance or spear or sharp-edge else I saw
Gripped or hanging from his fingered claw.

The avenue grew steeper as it fell,
Turning from a slope into a well.

I saw him raise his right arm in a fist,
Punching at the sky as down he fly.
Swirling 'round him came a smoky mist
Trailing in his wake as he came by.
A doleful shriek from deep within his soul
Cut the thickened air through canyon halls.
This mournful cry, unhuman in its make,
Dared to prod the dead to come awake.

Trammeling through the funerous black,
The cry was fugued across the ridges backs

The cry became a bell's clap in the air,
Cut from the broken and cracked-iron throat.
It chimed its dying song in devil's lair,
Turning to a single leaden note.
A somber silence lay upon the night,
A seething prelude stillness set to break.
This overture, the summons had put out,
And of a dire spirit's need did shout.

I saw a quiver on a distant ridge.
A man-shape stood near-naked in the night.
Against a pale sky on a stony bridge,
He set his outline in the fire's light.
The flames had tossed a sheet across the gloom,
A dully brightened masque of yellow gray.
It bounced upon the overhang of cloud,
Wrapping like a dingy iron shroud.

Upon another hill a winged thing,
Creeping like a lizard in the dirt.
Beside it did a wraith shape up and spring,
Summoned by my presence he assert.
Hollow eyes flecked out from midst the dark,
Staring as I follow in my course.
Feathered, gilled, and leathered hands arose;
Everywhere a being did enclose.

Movement tousled every hillock brake;
Each rock and rill coughed up the baleful beasts.
The mountains twist their back and upward shake
A thousand creatures and their pagan priests.
Legions lined upon the sloping's crest,
Two legged, four, and handless, clawed and winged.
They stood and watched me from their phalanx walls;
Not a cry or wail moved in the halls.

The multitude was waiting for command.
I watched my Self to find a rising hand.

He cried him out another croaking note,
Beying in the blackened mansion's room.
The single note upon the ether float,
A dying child within a withered womb.
A distant crescent hurled another chord,
Born in wretched bosom far away.
Another satyred minstrel struck his bow,
And painful whining from his heart out-flow.

The beastly canon tossed its mournful measure,
Trilling in discordant tuneless cant,
Piping out its brassy-baned displeasure
With cadence set to trolling, thrumming bant.
A shallow throated symphony blare out
From unstrung string and ever-broken brass.
The orchestral repetition set the chime,
But pounding, maudlin pounding set the rhyme.

A warbled lyric chorused from the clefts,
Screeched as if by dying moment's breath.
The singer snarled his note and sat bereft,
'Til new voice throated out the chant of death.
An army cackled out in the defile,
Calling to the cloaked man in the chase.
They flapped their wings and scratched their gnarled claws,
Cut their breast and at their stillness gnaw.

They droned a draining, straining call,
Beating on my senses with their strength.

Harsh and tuneless,
Pained and runeless,
Piped the throbbing pipers.

The demon symphony uplift;
It pitch and scaled its call.
Its orchest strained the melody,
The rhythm and the squall.

I fled it.
Dread it.
Outpaced the place to shed it.
But still the discord follow.

My mind grew weak.
Escape I seek.
But only down I run.

I couldn't turn,
I couldn't cry,
I closed my ears to sound.
But still they chant,
The demon rant.
The walls to shrill redowned.

Only downward comes to me.
Ever still the down.

The insolent valley swaggered down,
Plunging ever deeper in the chasm.
As stony tides lashed at its steepled crown,
Upon itself it turn in steely spasm.
The precipice collapsed into the valley,
Surging like a stone wave stopped in time.
Frozen granite leered into the air,
And reared its neck as if a rocky mare.

The runner in the distance raise his arm,
Casting over all the ghostly charm.

The demon army lurched down the decline,
Tramping from the ridge to where he lead.
They crawled and slithered from the mountain line,
Moving where my other Self decreed.
The sky was filled with legged and winged things,
Black against the hoar-frost, graying clouds.
They whirled and darted, carried by the gales,
Their wind-lift wings around them grimly flail.

All the bloodless beasts now follow me,
Not a one remaining on its perch.
Slavered tongues and wild-eyed things they be,
Everyone swept down to deathly church.
Trumpets spattered martial music there,
Drumming out a warrior's brew and bree.
The demon soldiers to the crypt a-light,
Reveling in its charnel house delight.

I scanned about this graveyard land,
This haunting, tombing, horrored vault,
Down the straight and down the thinning strand,
I dare not stop to think or fall or halt.
A moment s pause and ever I'm interred,
Buried 'neath these stony cataracts.
The pitchy fires brand and burn the rocks,
And char the boney mountains graying frocks.

In the fires phantom's face is seen
Of all the ones whose lives were lived unclean.

A mother's cry upon her infant's death,
Labors in my ear from distant place.
I hear her cry the failing of his breath,
And curse his life, her fortune, and disgrace.
Written in the flames two lovers cling
In violent and passionate embrace,
Consuming each the other with their flame.
Themselves they were consumed, consuming shame.

Upon a desert field a space apart,
The dead were want to calm their restless bones.
They picked their barren graves to hide their heart,
Burying themselves among the stones.
Naked, man and woman fell to earth,
Covered with 'the dung that was their life.
They rotted where they lay in ashen heap,
Joying in a dark unmurmured sleep.

The rites of death were all about me here,
Ugliness, deformity, too clear.

Phantoms, sprites, and elven-ghoulish spree
Pranced unbodied horrors all around.
They danced their scandaled steps in the debris;
Nameless terrors at their call abound.
My head grew dizzied, madness so nearby.
I barely kept my feet without a fall.
My pace grew frantic, bounding down the slope,
Pushing at the darkness as I grope.

The clouds had taken warring armies' form,
Battling on its gray and iron field.
Across its armored chest the forays storm,
Surging, swaying, thumping on the shield.
A mass of sordid silver crash another.
Cohorts locked and crushed formations front.
A wave of smoke ensmothered lesser tide,
Stamping opposition in its ride.

My heart was sunken, raving in its quest
To bridle the unholy in my breast.

My fleeing Self was still a space away.
Falling, crawling,
Spilling down and sprawling,
And still he paced away.

The margent to a single path
        had thinned.
Barren fields were no more to be seen
At left an ivory wall.
At right a jagged cleft.

Creatures clambered on the walls,
Where such as I not go.
They shrilled and cried,
Wilted, lilted, stilted cried,
And scratched to follow me.

I flew and leaped,
Raced and crept.
My pathway still behind.

'Til but a moment's running back
Was I.

He seemed to slow,
As if he know,
The chase was done its do.

Eerie lights of violet lit the path,
That leveled straight as damson decked the wrath.

He raced on for a moment and was lost,
Amidst the purple, plummish hue and haze.
The corridor with scar et stones embossed
Was lighted with an amethystine glaze.
The columned rock was gruesome in its shape,
Coarse and blemished in ungainly twist.
Disfigured were the too-forbidding walls,
That graceless sat and cordoned off the halls.

The temple massif billowed out and spread,
Becoming vernal chamber at its base.
The room was columned in a winish red,
Bowing in a circled, open space.
The pillared walls held only silvered sky.
Mottled marble veined this palace room.
Damask bathed the court in ghostly light,
Setting stilly like a violet night.

The other "I" stood 'cross the earthen floor,
Skulking in an eerie, spectral light.
He lurched and fretted, frantic all the more,
Now unhidden in the shaded night.
He roared and screeched and kicked the arid dust,
Raging that no passage was from here.
His back was bent, in full-unnatural crick,
Crooked down like a newly-broken stick.

He cursed and spat and seethed within this cell,
Where seemed he wanting all alone to dwell.

The odor of the dying pressed the air,
Swirling in this throne-room where we stand.
Thick and festered like the preyor's lair,
The rancid smell of illness crown this land.
A stench, too like a plague's scent struck me here,
Foulness fumed and lingered in this field.
The painful must abound of rotting flesh,
Which with the putrid, oily smells enmesh.

The creatures gathered on the ridging walls,
Looking down upon our manly shapes.
They perched and lined the mansion and the halls,
And rumored on the duelists, eyes agape.
Everything within this hell was here,
Following their leader to his throne.
They chirped and cried and roared at his command,
Summoned by his call and his demand.

He ruled the creeping things within this world;
Every devil's banner here unfurled.

I couldn't breathe for terror in my heart.
The sweat rushed out in sheet upon my face.
I never cared to learn the hero's art.
Mystery alone had led this chase.
My lips were shaking; no word from them came;
My hands pulled 'cross my face were wracked with fright.
Unarmed, came I. Unclad for such a match,
Trying not my darker soul to catch.

Eyes were blinded by a mist of tears,
Fountained by the creature's mocking jeers.

I wiped my eyes with fabric from my cloak,
Knowing that the combat matched us two.
The sweat I swept away with but a stroke.
I, courage for myself, from inward drew.
My hands I shook to shake away the quiver,
Knowing they must serve me well tonight.
I bent my knee to coil my body tight,
And clenched my fist 'til pressure drained it white.

My heart was pulsing, surging in its veins,
Summoning my daring to its place.
If death be mine than let my heart be slain,
And welcome death with grandeur on my face.
I came to see my features on this thing,
That led me to this hellish chamber here.
The killer's scroll was writ upon my eye,
I came to tell him once he was a lie.

He and I are not the same I dare;
Our single likeness is the face we bear.

The hare had turned and watched me standing still,
Poised to meet the demon in his den.
His head was twisted to the rocks and rill,
Smiling at the audience in the fen.
His cloak was rippled by the rankish wind.
His hands were empty, hanging at his side.
He stared at me with malice in his heart;
And every evil thought his face would chart.

The barely human flying things cry out,
Hawking for a newer kill,
The breaking of a mortal will,
        And new flesh for the pot.

The cauldrons rank,
The rottage stank.
Everywhere the clang.
The watchers cheer,
Their faces sneer,
Forwardly they hang.

My death, my death,
Humiliation, death,
        But first, humiliation.

An uproar swelled;
My dying knelled.
        Silently I stood.

They cheered and jeered,
Crashing in a mortal thrashing;
        All resistance dashing
        In my sinking flesh.

Beaked and creaked,
Clawed and double-jawed,
Crawing, gnawing beggars for my life.

I glanced around.
I weighed the sound.
Ten thousand eyes were mine.
Every one malignant,
My death their sole design.

Twenty pace away he raise his arm,
Lifting it within the purple mist,
To all his cohorts' signals, no alarm,
And motioned that their rancor they desist.
A silence fell across the demon mass;
Their assembly tilled their crying and their thrum.
No sound was uttered in this battle-place.
The prince had ordered silence of his race.

The air hung heavy in this theater round.
Alone were he and I upon the ground.

The arena's walls were littered with the beasts,
Gawking at my soul's infernal priest.

"There is no deeper," stepping forth, he say.
"Nowhere further may I flee your face."
I, wide-eyed, stood and watching him survey,
Saw him stalk me in this devilish place.
"This is the deepest pit within your soul,
Where I and all my demons make our land."
I struggled with my breath but came no sound,
Barely did my feet cling to the ground.

"Do you know me stranger?
Do you know my face?
Have you seen my eye?
Have you heard my laugh?"

He smiled at me that faithless, joyless smile,
That in the woods I saw within my rage.
He summoned all his venom and his bile,
While tossing me his challenge on this stage.
The twenty pace between us grew to less.
He swayed and pitched and nearer to me grew.
Our eyes were locked in heinous, dying duel,
One to win, one who came as fool.

Sweat was crusted thickly on his throat;
His bare chest swelling out with every breath.
Blood and gore his arms and legs were coat.
Every muscled bone was strained for death.
His fingers wrestled with the rankish air,
Twining, twisted, prodding in the haze.
The dagger at his hip gleamed in the shade,
Already dripping blood from killings made.

His voice was bristled like an unstrung bass,
Grinding on the grainy, half-swept strings.
He coughed his words in unconnected pace.
From leaden throat unthreaded bolts he flings.
His words wolfed out and crackled in the air,
Splitting to a shattered, shapeless sound.
He spoke as if deafness hold his ear.
Every word by muted mind he smear.

"Do you remember when you heard my foot
Trample in the grass so near beside.
Remember in your heart I laughing put
The hatreds that will bear you as their bride.
I would bring the darkness in your day.
I would roil your passions in the night.
Remember now the seethings in your soul,
When every kindness stealthily I stole."

He screamed and ranted, spitting out his words,
Cutting in my being as I heard.

He stamped and swaggered, throwing out his chest,
Prancing in the purple shaded light.
Shaking at my face with furored zest,
He scorched my mind, defiant in his might.
Exultant in bombastic resolution,
He tramped imposing step before the crowd.
Unfaltering he cowed my simple nerve,
Numbing it with his demonic verve.

He drew so near his breath lashed at my face,
Digging at my soul with poisoned glare.
I dare not look away or gaze unlace,
But met him with an icy-authored stare.
He burned his eyes into my mind's recess,
Tearing at my hopes and my design.
His red and violent eyes clawed at my heart,
Trying a confusion to impart.

My eyes raged back and leered into his soul,
And almost from its cradle evil stole.

His head began to shudder, eyes to quake.
His glance was broken casting it aside.
He grabbed his eyes and cringing at their ache,
Turned his head to hold his wounded pride.
He groaned a wailing, paining, injured cry,
Falling back and stumbling for a step.
He clutched his head and bared his gritted teeth,
And placed his hand upon his dagger's sheath.

The beasts blared out an uncontrolled reprise,
Startled at the master's lurching fall.
His faulter all the half-breeds he displease.
They rue his chink and roust about with gall.
He wiped his eye and ripped his pallid cheek,
Trying to regain his master's reign.
He thumped his chest and cursed my unmoved eye,
Leaping for the masse to join his cry.

A discord raged within the temple's court.
They clamored and his mastery exhort.

"Stranger," said the other Self to me,
"You follow me where no one ever go.
In deepest cavern in your soul you be,
Where I do rule and winds of evil blow."
His ragged finger pointed at my face;
Gnarled and crooked it quivered out at me.
"You have found, the devil in your soul.
With this Unknown your heart will not console."

"I am the hardness in your breast.
I am the coarseness in your touch.
I have stolen.
I have killed with you."

"Look at me, you fool!!!
Look at me!!!" He screamed.

"I am you.
    I am what you are."

A single tear fled shyly from my eye,
Rivered down and dropping from my cheek.
I wanted to accuse him of a lie,
But silence held my tongue when I would speak.
The tear came from a well so deep within,
Moistened from the wringings of my heart.
This single tear upon my face he see,
Knowing that the blow had staggered me.

"Ten thousand times you've seen me," he pipe out,
And circled me as quarry for his net.
Memories of me he hurl about,
Memories my soul tried to forget.
He waved his arm and phantoms fanned around,
Miming of the scenes I won't recall.
They danced and spun and showed my passing years,
Times that I'd remembered in my fears.

"Remember when you loved her in the wood,
Wrestling on your belly like a whore,
When neither of your passion was withstood,
And tied yourselves like mongrels on the floor.
I was with you then. You heard me there,
Laughing at your nakedness and shame.
You looked at her with my face not with yours,
And on your head my desecration pour."

I saw my shadow dancing with the maid,
Groaning, in the vision in the shade.
His mind careened of more.

"I was smiling when you trade your coins,
Each day within the marketplace at dawn,
When you the hawkers and the craftsmen join
Bazaaring and to selling places drawn.
I was with you when you slyly stole
The day's work of a craftsman at his task.
You kept your interest thieving by the law,
Giving less than what they rightly draw."

"You had lined your pockets with their toil,
Enriching but yourself while they despoil."

I saw the moneychangers in the clouds,
When the demons summoned them to dance.
I heard the coin and metal clinking loud,
Stealing every pence when had I chance.
Fortunes made I by my guile and ruse,
Fattening my purse in market square.
I heard his laughing then and smiled to hear
My demon soul then snick'ring in my ear.

I heard him then.
And knew him then.
But chased him not away.

His shallow eye was sparkling as he tell
How often I had journeyed to this hell.

"And when your love was spurned that single time
When woman would not have you to her bed,
Recall your planning hatred and your crime,
And when you wished her other lover dead.
You would have killed him like a cow for meal,
Squeezing out his life like rotted fruit.
Do you remember now you saw my face
When diabolic yearnings you embrace."

My single tear had ushered out a flood.
I wept as if my life had been a loss.
Every hope was drowning in the mud,
My little virtue hung upon his cross.
He and I had walked my life together,
Knowing yet unknowing he was there.
To inner-chambered heart he held the key.
More of me than I he seemed to be.

My breath fell out in gasps.
I coughed and spat.
My head was reeling,
Dizzy feeling,
Wanting to escape.

My eye was fixed upon him as he stalk,
Hounding me a scarce few feet away.
He slow-step rounding closer as he walk,
Hunting, shunting in the blackened clay.

He saw my tears,
My surging fears,
And laughed infernal laughter.
His hunter caught,
With terror fraught,
This fool who chased him after.

He scattered the clouds of visions,
With a circle of his hand,
Leaving snared the snarer
On this dark arena's sand.

The crowd pressed for my kill.
Cheering, jeering death, they cried their will.

"By a thousand cuts I'll kill you," said the fiend
"Slicing every vein with pricking blade.
Here you'll lie a corpse to lay demeaned.
Your life a token to my pride be paid."
His purpose was to smother goodness out,
Letting blossom wither on the vine,
To parch my soul until its dryness kill,
And in its place a demon conscience fill.

My arid tongue threw out a thread of words,
Whirling him around with questions heard.

"Have you parched my soul that it is yours?
Have you, courting, won my foolish trust?"
He turned and craned his neck to hear the more,
And listen to me whining in the dust.
"Am I yours?" I asked with falling eye.
My strength had fled and left me cringing there.
"I never welcomed you, or raised my hand,
Nor ever do your bidding or demand."

My mirror Self upraised his spine erect,
Stretching out its being to its length.
A fool's resistance in me he detect,
And wished to strangle out my waning strength.
"No. I never held you in my grasp.
Never, not a single time was mine.
You always chased me when you find my trace.
And here you be. Here. Staring at my face."

"Your soul was never mine, nor ever will.
You sang too well in moment's when alone.
The noble heart I couldn't win or kill,
Nor ever simple goodness I dethrone."
His hand ran to his dagger in his belt,
Tightening about its handle's back.
He then unsheathe its blade with blood a-drip,
And hold it in a slayer's deathly grip.

"I'd kill you in a subtle, sapping way,
But courage spoil my banter and my play."

"My being is to prosecute your death.
By many ways am I to still your breath."

He drew again to scarce arm's reach away,
The blade uplifted and poised to find my heart.
The stalker moved to clutch his mortal prey,
And to me timeless darkness to impart.
My eyes were fixed. I drew a weighty breath,
Frozen in my waiting for the strike.
A distant silence coursed within my brain,
Waiting to enfold me as the slain.

He pressed his face to mine and sneering hiss;
Before he struck he touched me in a kiss.

A melody cracked in my frigid mind,
Soaring in a lush and rhythmic tone.
A lyre wove its music and its line,
A thrilling cadence through my mind was thrown.

Pipers pitched their chords from darkest den,
Flooding every cavern in my thought.
The strains of songstress winds leaped in my towers,
Fluting through my templed garden's bowers.

Rich and flush the tunes blared out their notes,
Fuguing in a movement trilling clear.
A choral chant cut from a thousand throats,
Medlied in my heart's turned-inward ear.
Violins cascaded in their number,
Echoing within mind's chambered halls.
There soloed out a golden-hearted chime,
Repeating in its clangored, chanting rhyme.

From deep within my shivered soul there rumble,
Born a minstrel's tune I carried out,
Swelling in the dungeon walls it crumble,
A harmony my heart now quaking shout.
A troubadour laid lyric on my soul,
Hymning that my life still daring be.
The magic of a lullaby was wound,
Serenading every strength it found.

A symphony enchanted in its swelling.
The orchestra in hearts confinement strained.
Emotion from its fountain now was welling,
Bursting in the shackles that constrain.
Majesty was strumming with the chorus,
Trumpeting my life from psalming horns.
In my chapelled bosom joyous ringing,
Ten thousand voices choired in their singing.

The demon was as deafened to the song.
Music in these shadows not belong.

The blade was raised, his arm a tensing coil.
Into my eyes he blazed his brutish stare.
His lips were parted screaming to a boil.
Enmity would have its tortured share.
His eyes pursue me in my being's hollow,
Lunging at my soul with maliced threat.
I saw my face and all the horror there,
Refusing in the devil's heart to share.

I leaped and caught his wrist in downward plunge,
Lifting all my weight to hurl me out.
He, with the ruddy blade, still at me lunge,
Crying for my death with maddened shout.

We locked in rage,
And wracked the stage,
        Swirling on the earth.

His eye was red.
His hand was white.
        The veins strained at the skin.

I and I now struggle.
I and more than I.

We spit and kicked,
Ripped and twist,
This mirror and myself.

Was he more than I?
Was he more than I myself might be?

I hated my very face,
Contorted with an anger,
        Deeper than my soul.

The demons raged and clacked and clawed.
Their champion enthrall.
They cried in such malignant roar,
And furied in the hall.

A mystic cloud enwrapped the duel.
My mind was distant then.

Nature guided hand and arm,
And mortal strength it give.
Unchallenged was my death before.
But now I chose to live.

The melody within my soul
        Was pounding its refrain.
A noble chorus banged its chant,
        And with its power strain.

The blade was up.
Two hands were clasped,
        Pulling at the knife.

I thrust it down
When full I grasped.
        My Self surrendered life.

The knife blade stood up-right within his chest,
And cut a space beneath his smattered throat.
He heaved and then a stillness struck his breast.
Blood with sanguine pen his dying wrote.
I lay upon him clinging to the knife;
Both hands holding to its bloodied shaft.
To see my deathly eyes I cast my glance,
And see him, open-eyed, in frozen trance.

I tensed and shuddered limp.

A silence, struck in disbelief, abound.
The creatures in their demon work were stilled.
Their king by manly being was uncrowned;
And with a stave their master had been killed.
Gawking from the ridging canyons walls,
They stared wild-eyed upon the battle's ground.
Their blinking eyes were slashing through the shade,
Upon their chieftain, where his body laid.

I rolled from on his body to the ground,
Lying in the dust and clinging clay.

I lay there lumpish like a block of coal,
Unmindful of my pain and of my hurt.
It seemed as if I'd killed my very soul,
Looking on this dead hulk in the dirt.

Its eyes were staring blankly at the sky.
Open-jawed and mud-caked was its face.
I moved my fingers pulling eye-lids shut,
Wiping rubied blood smears from its cut.

The rankish scent of death was in the breeze.
Morbid clung the odor to the ground.
I lift myself and climb up to my knees,
Raising up my head to scan around.
The beasts in utter silence held their place,
Faces painted with bewildered look.
Their eyes were staring, ripping from their head,
Unwarned and unprepared for this instead.

A scarcely human shape with fang-like arms,
Perched upon the farthest distant ridge,
It turned its back from this arena's harms,
And shuttled off across a stony bridge.
It disappeared into the mountain's clefts,
The first departing from the bouldered depths.
Another winged creature cut the air,
Returning to its dungish, rotted lair.

The beastly viewers then did skulk away,
Chastened that their master had been slain.
They passed in silent columned disarray,
From near the stage where demon's Self was lain.
With silent step they crossed the sharp defile,
Passing the escarpments as they go.
No voice did even murmur in retreat,
One sound alone, and that of dragging feet.

Soon I was alone in templed pit,
Alone, but for this killing I commit.

Who killed I in this bout in darkness' realm?
Whose face lay on the corpse that lie so dead?
From where had come my strength to overwhelm,
And snatch the knotted garland from his head?
I had not sought his death but he sought mine,
Wanting my destruction as his prize.
Had I killed the killer in my soul?
Have I lost a part or am I whole?

If this is what I am than let it die.
Better dead than seething in my heart.
What he is my being must defy,
And if he's mine, I tear away his part.
There was no joy to see my body dying,
Impaled upon the knife stock in my breast.
The horror in the face was blanked and shattered.
Malignance in his life, it seemed, was scattered.

I tried to weep but tears were gone and dry,
This moment's solace to the dead deny.

I left the court and climbed the narrow halls,
Leading from the sulfured, hellish cell.
I paced along the canyon's murky walls,
That corridored the path to private hell.
The vaults of stone declined and dulled their ridges,
Sweeping from their mountains to a field.
The umbered heavens strained upon their chain,
Tossed their shoulders and their leaden mane.

I climbed 'til dawn when claret-grandeur broke,
And flood the verdant plains with flaunting glow.
It threw across the sky its azure cloak,
And bounced its diamond paint on river's flow.
The gilded saffron lilies danced their step,
Upon the emerald carpet 'neath my feet.
The russet trees cast out their bountied shade,
Freckling all the pastures and the glade.

It tripped and gamboled,
danced and rambled,
    In the warming sun.
Bucking, spinning,
Romping, grinning,
    In caressing sun.

I capered in the violet and the blue,
The green and tawny, checkered and the hue,
Fawn brown,
Blue-gowned,
    Pied and hilted, opaline and quilted.

Hazel-nutted,
Pearly-shutted,
Every line, and wind, and flush.

In a clump of thorny bush I see
My moaning, beaten body thieves had rob.
I looked and recognized an anguished me,
Clutching at my wounds with mewling sob.
He cursed and kicked, blaspheming at the thieves,
Mourning every wound he suffered-then.
His misery and wretched mind were pained,
So every god and goddess he profaned.

He cried about his coin and missing gold,
And all that with their loss the Fates withhold.

He whined of how they caught him unaware,
And vengeance for his injuries he swear.

We stood but body's length away;
But me he couldn't see.
He wrestled with the thicket's web
That tangled 'round his knee.

Tragedy was etched upon his face,
A poverty he, foolish, didn't see.
His honor by indignity displace.

His hatreds by his greedy heart decree.
He wore the masque I former wore myself.
Our dress was still the same as was before.
The avarice of much-corrupted life
Wrought in him a bitter, sorrowed strife.

I saw this mangled, cheerless man I knew,
And grieved that he was me as I was known,
Who every tender gentleness he slew,
Strangling gracious charities half-grown.
Had I come back to join this prideful soul,
And pass my days in vanity and boast?
Once again my face tormented me,
When, as I was, a loathsome wretch I see.

The sun was laying gentle on my shoulder,
Pressing on my cheek a warming kiss.
This wounded heart was chilled and growing colder,
So soon to fall into the vile abyss.
My eyes I turned from burdening affliction
That labored to unsnare its stranded self.
The winsome air enraptured with its flagrance,
And drew me from this mire with its fragrance.

My face no longer pains me when I look.
A mirror sees me smile in gentle way.
My eyes can gaze in tenderness upon you,
Healing when my life around you play.

My wretched heart no more my life subbornes.
I left it where I found it, in the thorns.

Milton Keynes UK
Ingram Content Group UK Ltd.
UKHW022322051024
449173UK00003B/25